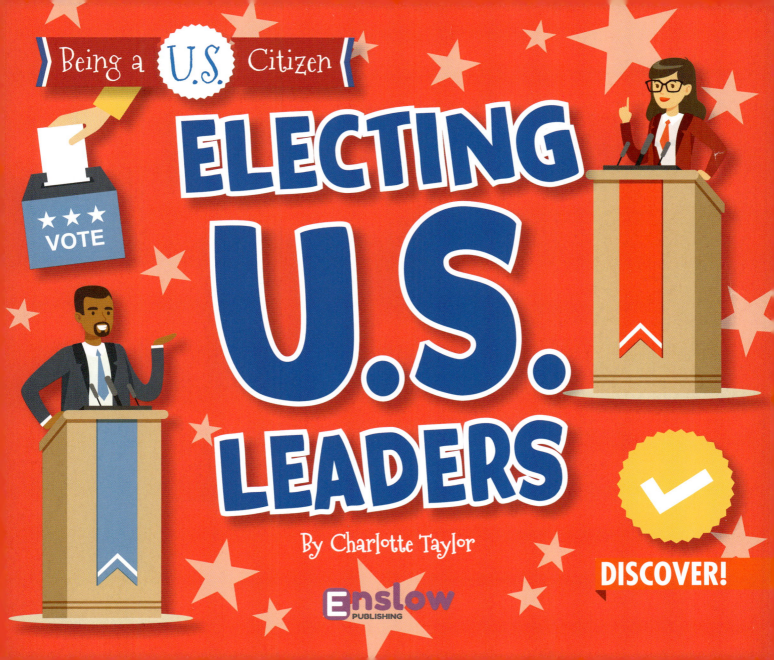

Please visit our website, www.enslow.com. For a free color catalog of all our high-quality books, call toll free 1-800-398-2504 or fax 1-877-980-4454.

Library of Congress Cataloging-in-Publication Data

Names: Taylor, Charlotte, author.
Title: Electing U.S. leaders / Charlotte Taylor.
Description: New York : Enslow Publishing, 2021. | Series: Being a U.S. citizen | Includes index. | Contents: Words to know – Hear our voice! – Who are the leaders? – The voters – The history of voting – The candidates – The campaign – Election Day – And the winner is... – For more information.
Identifiers: LCCN 2019050698 | ISBN 9781978517455 (library binding) | ISBN 9781978517431 (paperback) | ISBN 9781978517448 (6 Pack) | ISBN 9781978517462 (ebook)
Subjects: LCSH: Elections–United States–Juvenile literature. | Voting–United States–Juvenile literature. | United States–Politics and government–Juvenile literature.
Classification: LCC JK1978 .T39 2020 | DDC 323.60973–dc23
LC record available at https://lccn.loc.gov/2019050698

Published in 2021 by
Enslow Publishing
101 West 23rd Street, Suite #240
New York, NY 10011

Copyright © 2021 Enslow Publishing

Designer: Laura Bowen
Editor: Megan Quick

Photo credits: Cover, pp. 1 (ballot, check mark), 7 (Capitol building), 8 (ballot box), 16 (debate art), 19 (check mark) Alexander Ryabintsev/Shutterstock.com; cover, pp. 1, 14 (politicians) NotionPic/Shutterstock.com; pp. 4 (girl), 13 (boy), 20 (boy), 21 (balloons) ann131313/Shutterstock https://www.nps.gov/articles/voting-rights-in-nj-before-the-15th-and-19th.htm.com; p. 5 kali9/Shutterstock.com; p. 7 mark reinstein/Shutterstock.com; p. 9 adamkaz/Shutterstock.com; p. 10 (suffragette) SofiaV/Shutterstock.com; p. 11 Everett Historical/Shutterstock.com; p. 12 (money) Quarta/Shutterstock.com; p. 13 William Lovelace/Stringer/Hulton Archive/Getty Images; p. 15 SDI Productions/Shutterstock.com; p. 17 Trong Nguyen/Shutterstock.com; p. 19 Hill Street Studios/DigitalVision/Getty Images; p. 21 Jupiterimages/PHOTOS.com>>/Getty Images Plus/Getty Images.

Portions of this work were originally authored by Earl McGraw and published as *Electing Our Leaders*. All new material in this edition was authored by Charlotte Taylor.

All rights reserved. No part of this book may be reproduced in any form without permission in writing from the publisher, except by a reviewer.

Printed in the United States of America

Some of the images in this book illustrate individuals who are models. The depictions do not imply actual situations or events.

CPSIA compliance information: Batch #BS20ENS: For further information contact Enslow Publishing, New York, New York, at 1-800-398-2504.

Find us on

CONTENTS

Hear Our Voice!...........................4
Who Are the Leaders?..................6
The Voters..................................8
The History of Voting.................10
The Candidates.........................14
The Campaign...........................16
Election Day..............................18
And the Winner Is....................20
Words to Know.........................22
For More Information...............23
Index.......................................24

Boldface words appear in Words to Know.

HEAR OUR VOICE!

Have you ever had a vote in your classroom? Each person in the class gets to say what they want. They have a voice. In the United States, we vote to **choose** our leaders. Every American **citizen** has a voice.

YOU CAN VOTE TO NAME THE CLASS PET OR DECIDE WHAT GAME TO PLAY.

WHO ARE THE LEADERS?

Leaders help make our rules and laws. They might be leaders of cities, towns, or states. In an **election**, we can choose many different kinds of leaders. The leader of the country is the president. We vote for president every four years.

LEADERS FROM AROUND THE COUNTRY WORK IN WASHINGTON, DC.

U.S. CONGRESS

THE VOTERS

Not everyone can vote! You have to be 18 years old. You must also be a U.S. citizen. This means you were born in the United States or you became a citizen another way. You also have to sign up, or register, to vote.

PEOPLE CAN VOTE IN ELECTIONS EVERY YEAR.

THE HISTORY OF VOTING

When the country began, only white men could vote. Most women and people of different races could not vote. This was unfair. They had to fight for the right to vote. Black men got the right to vote in 1870.

ALL WOMEN GOT THE RIGHT TO VOTE IN 1920.

For a long time, it was very hard for black citizens to vote. They had to pay money to vote. Many did not have enough money, so they could not vote. This finally changed in 1965.

THE CANDIDATES

The people who run in elections are called **candidates**. They all want to get the most votes. Candidates make speeches to tell us their ideas. A speech is a long talk in front of other people.

A CANDIDATE HAS TO ANSWER LOTS OF QUESTIONS.

THE CAMPAIGN

People decide whom to vote for by listening to the candidates. The candidates meet with many people. They put ads on TV. They use **social media**. They also take part in **debates**. This is when they talk about their ideas with the other candidates.

AT ELECTION TIME, THERE ARE MANY SIGNS WITH THE NAMES OF CANDIDATES.

ELECTION DAY

Finally, Election Day arrives! People go to schools or other **public** buildings to vote. They may go into a voting **booth**. Voting is usually done on a machine or on paper. Some people mail in their votes. This way is slower, but it still works.

VOTING BOOTHS KEEP EVERYONE'S VOTE A SECRET.

AND THE WINNER IS...

Many people count all of the votes. They have help from computers. If it's close, sometimes the votes are counted again! The person with the most votes wins. The right to vote is an important part of being an American citizen.

WORDS TO KNOW

booth A small, closed space.

candidate Somebody who runs in an election.

choose To pick.

citizen Someone who lives in a country legally and has certain rights.

debate An argument or discussion in front of other people.

election The act of choosing a leader.

public Open to all people.

social media Websites and applications (apps) made to bring people together online.

FOR MORE INFORMATION

Books

Czajak, Paul. *Monster Needs Your Vote.* Minneapolis, MN: Mighty Media Kids, 2015.

Worth, Bonnie. *One Vote, Two Votes, I Vote, You Vote.* New York, NY: Random House, 2016.

Websites

PBS Kids: You Choose
pbskids.org/youchoose
Watch videos and play games as you learn about voting.

United States Government: How Voting Works
www.ducksters.com/history/us_government_voting.php
Find out more about how elections work.

Publisher's note to educators and parents: Our editors have carefully reviewed these websites to ensure that they are suitable for students. Many websites change frequently, however, and we cannot guarantee that a site's future contents will continue to meet our high standards of quality and educational value. Be advised that students should be closely supervised whenever they access the internet.

INDEX

ads, 16

black men/citizens, 10, 12

campaigns, 16

candidates, 14, 16

citizens, 4, 8, 12, 20

counting votes, 20

debates, 16

Election Day, 18

elections, 6, 14

ideas, 14, 16

laws, 6

leaders, 4, 6

president, 6

social media, 16

speeches, 14

voters, 8

voting, 4, 6, 8, 10, 12, 18, 20

voting rights, 10, 12

women, 10